Bird-Watching

By Margaret Carney

CELEBRATION PRESS
Pearson Learning Group

Contents

Why Watch Birds?

Have you ever seen a hawk dive like a speeding arrow? Have you watched ducks marching in a line? Have you observed a pair of birds busily building a nest? If so, you know why bird-watching is so popular.

Bird-watchers can learn a great deal about birds by studying them in their **habitats**. By looking and listening, they learn to identify birds by their appearance, behavior, and songs. Bird-watchers also help scientists by gathering and sharing their information. If you would like to become a bird-watcher, this book can get you started.

Hummingbirds can fly backward.

The kookaburra often sounds like a person laughing.

Some swans live to be seventy years old.

Finding Birds

You can find birds in all kinds of habitats, ranging from open areas to crowded cities. Birds usually live in fields, deserts, high grasses, trees, bushes, parks, and near water. You can find the birds in your area with the help of a **field guide**. A field guide tells you what **species** of birds live near you, what types of habitats they live in, and what time of year the birds are in your area.

Eurasian jay feeding in the woods, Scotland

pigeons in the city, Croatia

geese in a pond, Canada

rosella in grassland, Australia

Materials
- a field guide
- a notebook
- a pencil or a pen

1 Borrow a field guide from a library or a friend, or buy one at a bookstore. Some field guides cover only one region or country, so make sure your field guide includes your area.

2 Look for the **range maps** in your field guide. In some guides, they are all located in one section. In other guides, there is a range map next to each bird.

3 Choose a bird that lives in your country and find the range map for that bird. If your location is shaded or colored, the bird may live in or around your area.

Canada

United States

Mexico

N
W E
S

Map Key

summer months

all year round

This range map shows where the osprey lives in North America.

osprey

Turn the page to continue this activity. ☞

Migration

Some birds **migrate** from place to place. Others live in the same area all year. If a bird migrates, the range map may be shaded with two colors or patterns. Use the map key to find out what time of year each color or pattern represents.

osprey
nesting

4 Make a list of other birds that you would like to find that are in your area during this time of year.

5 Add the habitats of these birds, such as trees, shrubs, fields, ponds, and beaches, to your list.

3 Take a hat with a brim to keep the sun out of your eyes so that you can see the birds clearly.

4 Wear sunscreen and take insect repellent with you if you're bird-watching during warm months.

5 Bring a notebook and colored pencils or pens so you can keep a bird journal. (The next activity will show you how.)

6 Make sure you have your field guide and your binoculars with you.

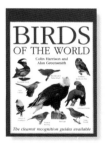

7 Pack a bottle of water and a snack. If you plan to spend the day hiking, take a lunch. Now you're ready for bird-watching!

Watching Birds

When you go bird-watching, you should take a bird journal. A bird journal is a notebook where you write about the birds that you see. This will help you remember them and better understand their habits. Here's how to keep a bird journal while you are bird-watching.

MY BIRD JOURNAL

Materials
- a notebook
- colored pencils or pens

1 Write down the date, time, and location where you first see each bird. Also, make a note about what the weather is like.

2 Use your binoculars to study the bird up close. Remember to use the controls to help you focus on the bird.

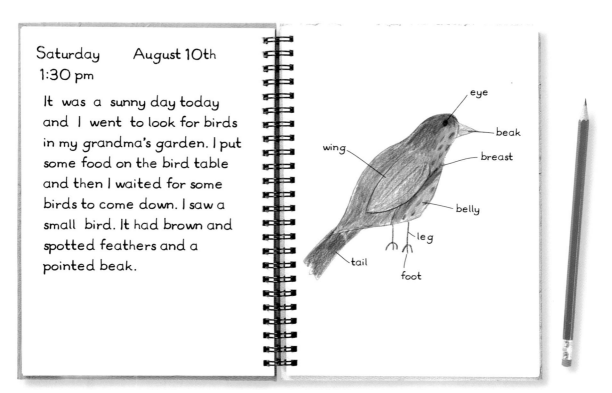

Saturday   August 10th
1:30 pm

It was a sunny day today
and I went to look for birds
in my grandma's garden. I put
some food on the bird table
and then I waited for some
birds to come down. I saw a
small bird. It had brown and
spotted feathers and a
pointed beak.

eye
beak
wing
breast
belly
leg
tail
foot

3 Write about what you see. Describe the bird's appearance, such as its size, color, beak shape, wings, or kind of feet. If you do not recognize the bird, compare it with a bird that you know. For example, is it larger than a robin? Is its beak hooked like a hawk's or pointed like a sparrow's?

4 Make a sketch of the bird. Draw any special **field markings**, or colors and feather patterns, that you see on the bird.

thrush

Turn the page to continue this activity. ☞

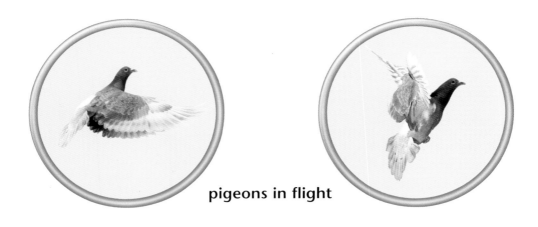

pigeons in flight

5 Write down how the bird moves. When it flies, does it glide or flap its wings? Does it travel in a **flock**, with a partner, or alone? Does it walk, hop, or climb?

6 Describe any other activities or behaviors that you observe. For example, is the bird eating seeds or insects? Is it **preening** its feathers?

azure kingfisher feeding

7 Listen for any songs or calls made by the bird. Each species has its own. For example, are the bird's calls raspy, or clear and whistling? Describe these sounds in your journal.

macaws preening

8 Use your journal and a field guide to identify the species of each bird that you see. (The next activity will show you how.)

white crowned sparrow singing

Identifying Birds

Once you have finished writing information in your journal, it's time to identify the bird that you saw. You may want to follow these steps while you are still out in the field. You may also compare your bird journal notes to the field guide when you return home.

Parts of a Bird

crown

beak or bill

chin

back

eye

wing

throat

rump

breast

tail

side

leg

belly

foot

Perhaps you will see a Eurasian robin, like this one, when you go bird-watching.

Materials
- a field guide
- your bird journal

1 Find the picture in the field guide that looks most like the bird that you saw.

2 Compare the picture and the bird's description to your journal notes and what you remember about the bird. If you are unsure of what part of a bird the guide is referring to, check the labels on the bird diagram on page 16, or near the front of your field guide.

Turn the page to continue this activity. ☞

I saw four small birds in the park today. They all looked the same. They had brown and gray feathers and some had white stripes on their wings. They all had short, sharp beaks.

common sparrow

Bird Beaks

You can identify birds by the shape of their beaks. The beak's shape can tell you what type of food the bird eats and how it gets its food. Here are some examples.

▶ A short, pointed beak helps the silver-eared mesia crack open small seeds.

▶ A sharp, hooked beak helps the golden eagle tear meat.

▶ A long, thin beak helps the gray-breasted spiderhunter snatch spiders from their webs.

▶ A wide, flat beak helps the white duck strain small animals, plants, and seeds from water.

3 Check the range map to see if that bird ever appears in your area. If it doesn't, you are probably looking at a bird that is similar to the one in your field guide, but is actually a different bird.

4 Check in the field guide for the time of year or the season when the bird is found in your area. Does the bird live in your area all the time or only during one season? See if this information matches when you saw the bird.

5 Write the name of the bird in your journal.

Soon you'll know birds common to your neighborhood. Don't worry if you can't identify every bird. Even experts can become confused. Trying to identify birds is just part of the fun of bird-watching.

Unidentified Birds

If you're not sure about the identity of your bird, check your notes carefully. Could the bird be a **juvenile**? Juveniles, or young birds, have different **plumage**, or feathers, than adult birds. Some birds' plumage changes in winter, too. Also, don't forget that in some bird species, the males and females look different.

male greenfinch

female greenfinch

juvenile greenfinch

Making a Bird Feeder

Bring the birds to you by making this simple bird feeder. If you hang a bird feeder near a window, you can study birds up close without scaring them. Ask an adult to help you.

Materials
- a pencil
- a half-gallon cardboard milk or juice carton
- strong scissors
- a large nail
- sunflower seeds
- sturdy string or wire, 2 to 3 feet long

1 Draw a square on one side of the carton, about two inches from the bottom of the carton. Next, cut along only two sides of the square.

2 Cut across the middle of the square to make two flaps. Fold one flap up and fold the other one down.

3 Repeat the first two steps on the opposite side of the carton.

4 Reach inside the carton and carefully poke holes in the bottom with the nail. The holes will allow rainwater to drain out.

5 Poke a large hole in the top of the carton. Then thread the string or a wire through the hole.

7 Tie the feeder to a tree or porch rafter. Watch who comes to eat. It might take a while for the birds to find the feeder, so be patient. Remember to clean out the feeder and replace the seeds every few weeks.

6 Put sunflower seeds in the feeder.

Feeding Birds

Be careful about what foods you put in your bird feeder. Salty foods are harmful to birds and should never be left for them. Sunflower seeds, millet, and thistle seeds are good. Many birds also like to eat suet, a hard animal fat.

sunflower seeds

suet cone

Joining a Bird Count

With practice, you'll soon become an expert bird-watcher. Something else may happen, as well. Most bird-watchers come to appreciate birds deeply. Some even help scientists who study bird populations.

Several organizations hold yearly bird counts. These events involve thousands of people across the country. They work in groups to count the total number of birds they see in a specific area on a single day. The counts are combined and fed into computers. Scientists can then tell which bird populations grow or decline from year to year. If you'd like to join a bird count, write to the address or visit the Web site on this page for more information.

magpie

Bird Count Contact Information

Project FeederWatch
Cornell Lab of Ornithology
159 Sapsucker Woods Road
Ithaca, New York 14850
http://birds.cornell.edu/pfw

Glossary

binoculars	a tool that magnifies objects at a distance
calls	sounds that a bird makes to communicate with other birds
field guide	a reference book that helps readers identify things found in nature
field markings	the color, marks, or feather patterns on a bird that distinguish it from other birds
flock	a group of birds that lives, eats, and travels together
habitats	places where plants and animals naturally live
juvenile	a young, immature animal
magnify	to make something look larger and closer
migrate	to move from one place to live in another
pishing	pushing air through the teeth to make a loud, whispering sound that attracts birds
plumage	the feathers on a bird
preening	smoothing and arranging of feathers by a bird
range maps	maps that show the area where an animal can be found at different times of the year
species	one specific kind of plant or animal

Index